Cley

Seasons to be Cheerful

isbn 978-1-910001-19-6

Cley, Seasons To Be Cheerful

first edition

published by

Red Hare Publishing Ltd
c/o Pinkfoot, High St,
Cley NR25 7RB
www.redharepublishing.co.uk

proud to be printing in Britain
with www.swallowtailprint.co.uk

Cley

Seasons to be Cheerful

Sarah Whittley

This is a book for anyone who loves Cley and the North Norfolk Coast. My childhood memories of Cley are happy ones as we were only here on holiday, maybe that's why I always wanted to move here. But I think it's more likely that it's because Cley is one of the most beautiful places I've visited in England. The following pages are my photographic record of the landscape and wildlife I crave everyday. Although I've been taking photographs for many years, I'm not a professional photographer but I have a good camera and I try to get out when the light is good. I love taking pictures in misty, sea fret conditions and, as I'm sure you'll notice, I love taking pictures of cows. The criteria for what to include in this book is if I can walk or cycle from Cley. I wanted to organise this book by the seasons to show how stunning Cley is all year round. I hope it's worked.

WINTER
december january february

There's much to celebrate in Cley during these months. With snow and sleet statistically more likely to fall in spring, our North Norfolk winters are much maligned. Big winter skies, crisp bright frosty mornings and blinding sunshine make winter in Cley a naturalist's delight. The highlight has to be the tens of thousands of wintering geese that visit us from their Arctic breeding grounds. Vast skeins of Pink-footed Geese and Dark-bellied Brents fill the marshes and skies. They start appearing towards the end of September and by November you certainly know they're here. The Pinkfeets' unmistakable high-pitched, squeaky honks can be heard all around the village and on the reserve.

We play host to a massive collection of birds escaping the Arctic winter, from the truly wild Snow and Lapland Buntings, thousands of duck, including Wigeon and Teal, a vast array of waders to the smaller perching birds, like thrushes and Robins – Cley looks after them all. Not to forget our Grey Seals on Blakeney Point, which has recently become the largest breeding colony in England. A staggering 2,426 pups were born during the winter of 2014.

But probably the best thing about winter is that you can experience all of this and nine times out of ten, you'll be completely on your own. The deserted coast is left to hardy birders and walkers and of course, the birds.

top row *Views from Daukes Hide, Cley NWT Reserve* I remember having to cover my face from the cold on this biting January morning. You can see the northerly wind direction from the bent reeds and ruffled water.

bottom left *Brent Geese, NWT Cley* They arrive late afternoon to wash and brush up after a hard day at work feeding on winter cereal crops. You hear them first; far-carrying guttural purring 'ggrrrs, ggrrrs'. bottom right *Cley Harbour* A stock-still, frozen February morning at Cley's hidden harbour.

Sunrise from Daukes Hide, Feburary A very welcome sun rose over Pat's Pool and my hands began to thaw. After almost blinding myself from the rising sun's reflections on the snow, I moved on to Bishop's Hide (just visible to the right of this picture) to see if I could find anything alive .

Allan-Williams Gun Turret A crispy February walk to the beach this morning. As a child we played in this dome, never giving much thought to its origin. It's only since moving here I discovered it was made in 1940 for two soldiers to fire machine guns through. The top rotated 360 degrees and the aim was to protect Cley from a possible beach invasion. If only we'd known – it could have added a whole new dimension to our games.

9am On Cley Reserve, February

top and left *February, Towards Blakeney Freshes* A couple of minutes walk and I'm right on the Norfolk Coast Path. I try to be there most mornings, on the stretch from Cley to Blakeney. February light is full of icy blues and Naples yellows. Sadly the 2013 surge tide destroyed the red stand of trees seen top right.

above A scene you'll see frequently throughout this book. I've referred to it as Rachel's Ditch, as it's a view she often sketches. I always stop to see who's there, usually the only thing I see is the white flick of a Moorhen's rear end disappearing into the reeds.

Kestrel, Blakeney Freshes, December I can only imagine how cold this fluffed up Kestrel must have been. I had a fleece, lined trousers, hat, scarf and gloves, and I was still cold.

top *Cley Sluice, River Glaven* and *Glossy Ibis with Curlew, January* I have to walk by the sluice on my way to the Coast Path, there are usually one or two swans to say good morning to. top right An unexpected visitor this morning in the field just to the right of the river. The Glossy Ibis stayed in the area for a few weeks, befriending the resident Curlews.

bottom *Norfolk Coast Footpath, Cley* Once the Environment Agency have cut back the Alexanders, the path looks stark. I know it has to be done but it's sad to see the valuable over-wintering invertebrate life they support destroyed. *Whiffling Pink-footed Geese, February* The excitable, squeaky high-pitched cries of these wild geese is a soundtrack I'll never tire of hearing.

top *Roe Deer in the Snow* A visiting deer near the village in search of food.
above *Hunting Barn Owl* It's now rare to walk on the marshes in the evening
without seeing a hunting Barn owl. This one passes by the mill almost every night.
For every 'drop down' I see, about 1 in 7 are successful, resulting in a Field Vole.
But it hasn't always been the case here. The run of bad winters (2009–2011) and
the wet June of 2012 had a devastating effect on our local population.

15

top *Photographing Salthouse Snow Buntings with Robin, February* I couldn't refuse a trip out with a real photographer, Robin Chittenden, especially as it was to watch these special birds from the wild and remote parts of the high Arctic. They arrive in late September and sadly leave us in March. Sometimes they're so tame you wonder if they've ever seen a human before.

bottom *Turnstones, Salthouse* An added bonus today.

right *Snow Buntings, Salthouse* Before the surge tide, Salthouse car park was a good place to watch these beautiful birds. Now the car park has gone, the birds are more tricky to find. They wobble and creep along the shingle, blending is so well at first you think it's the shingle that's moving. Every year they winter in Norfolk and can be found combing shingle beaches for food, bringing a touch of real Tundra wilderness to our shores.

top *Walking Home, Cley* The familiar sight of walkers floating above the reeds on the beach footpath. left Cley Old Hall and the Mill were just about visible on this soft December morning.

From Old River Glaven, Cley Beach I took this picture late morning in February. The soft throaty gurglings of Brent geese rose from the dark marsh. I waited for the sun to move out of the cloud to give enough light to lift the mud to reveal the patterns within. This is the old river course before it was realigned 200m inland in 2006 to stop the shingle from filling the river during surge tides.

Rachel's Ditch, Blakeney Freshes, December I can't walk by this spot without lifting my camera, it will appear many times in this book. It only takes two minutes to reach on the Coast Path from Cley but technically it is Blakeney Fresh Marsh

right *Brent Geese & Boats in February, Cley Beach*

top *View Over the Reserve to Blakeney Point from Walsey Hills, Cley*
A wonderful location to get a scale of the vastness of the surrounding
landscape. Owned by the Norfolk Ornithological Association, this
three acre reserve is a real gem. Bishop's Hide is in the foreground.

left *Heron Club, February* This morning we watched the unfortunate
spawning frogs in the pool by East Bank being picked off by up to
ten hungry herons.

top *Daukes Hide with Blakeney Point Sand Hills, January*
right *Daukes Hide Under Water in the December 2014 Surge Tide.*
I took this the morning after the surge; the tops of Daukes Hides are
just visible. Thanks to the sluice system on the reserve, the harmful
saltwater was able to drain off the freshwater marsh within days.

Cley Old Hall, with Guard Dog Even though I pass this dog every time I walk
to the beach, it always makes me jump. Particularly so on this misty morning.

River Glaven from Cley Sluice, 10.35, February There could have been a spell on the land this morning - so still, only the trickle of water from the sluice and the occasional goose honking overhead.

Halfway House, River Glaven, December The sun had yet to burn off the frost from the banks of the Glaven. Thin sheets of pale blue ice covered red-brown muddy marsh pools. No birds, no sounds this cold, cold morning.

Looking Towards Blakeney Church from the Beach Another February morning with extraordinary light. I was the only person crunching through the shingle towards the Point – this view was all mine.

Waiting for the Sun I couldn't face disturbing these winter plumaged Black-headed gulls, they looked so relieved the sun had arrived to warm their bones on this teeth-chatteringly cold morning.

Norfolk Reeds, First Morning Light After autumn's pomegranate-coloured reed heads, by February it's as if all life and colour has been sucked from the reedbeds. Even though the cold wind had numbed my ears and nose, I couldn't move. I think these swaying reeds were actually hypnotising me.

left *Wigeon Pool, Blakeney Freshes*
On the last stretch of coast path before Blakeney, in the distance I saw Wigeon dropping from the sky and disappearing into the marsh by the Manor House Hotel. I heard the males far-carrying, wheezing whistle calls long before I found them again.

right *Brent Geese on a Dewy Marsh*

top *Morston Quay, February 10.20am*
Just the popping and crackling of drying mud, the splashes from a bathing gull and the Brents' gentle 'ggrrr' contact calls.
left *The House on the Hill, Morston*

Morston Quay, February Harsh Light

top *Wiveton Church, Late Afternoon Mist*
top right *Wiveton Church from Glandford Road* A walk to Wiveton in early December with rolling mist over the river Glaven. In winter, large flocks of foraging Curlew roam the meadows.

bottom left *Willows from Wiveton Bridge* It doesn't take long to walk to Wiveton; it helps having two pubs en route and the knowledge that whatever the weather, the views from the medieval stone bridge will be breathtaking.
above *Sunflower Seedheads, near Wiveton*

Coastguard Cottages, Weybourne 4.30, February

Somewhere Between Holkham & Wells, January Late afternoon watching the disappearing sunshine catch the receding tide on this vast cathedral of a beach. The only thing to worry about is how to get home.

Last Light in Wells Woods, January   The child in me surfaces every time I visit these woods. I want to climb the warped, gnarled pines and play Tarzan on the rope swing. You can walk to Wells from Cley along the Norfolk Coast Path, it can take around 3.5 hours but it always takes me a lot longer - too many things to see.

The Surge Tide, 5th December 2013 I wasn't sure whether to include images of this nerve-wracking night. But it happened and the next morning I was out with my camera recording the damage. The saddest thing was the jumble of hundreds of dead animals that died in the night. The Coast Path between Cley and Blakeney suffered around 30 complete breaches, flooding the fresh marsh with destructive saltwater. Fortunately for Cley the sea wall held.

Dead Hare, Norfolk Coast Path, Cley Tragically the hares I've watched on the Freshes over the years all perished that night. Such was the power of the surge, there was simply no escape. Amongst the carnage I found many dead freshwater fish, Water Rails, Moorhens, Field Voles, Reed Buntings and a Stoat. The saltwater was trapped on the fresh marsh for around 20 days, poisoning everything it covered.

top *The Coast Road the morning after the Surge Tide* We spent an anxious evening worrying if the tide would get over the bump in the road and rush down the High Street. Little did we realise it had breached Blakeney fresh marshes at the other end of the village. top right *The Coast Road Under Water* Dead freshwater fish floated down the road and displaced Water Voles scrambled on to the verge. A seal was seen swimming along the Coast Road, even making the national newspapers.

bottom left *The Morning After The Surge* I was one of the many dazed residents wandering around the village the following morning. The next tide was at 7am, it was high but nothing in comparison to the night before. botton right *Salthouse Shingle Ridge Breach* Salthouse Beach was unrecognisable, the sea tore through the shingle, forming a mini estuary overnight. Several weeks later, men in suits were still scratching their heads as to what to do. Luckily nature had the answer and the following tides fixed the breach.

SPRING
march april may

My excitement at the arrival of warmer weather and longer days are often scuppered by a cruel March, with achingly cold north winds and driving grey icy rain, sleet or snow – sometimes all three.

When spring finally arrives (astronomically it starts on the 20th March) it can bring some spectacular weather. As the air warms over the sea and hits the cooler land, sea frets or haars can appear within seconds. These cold wet mists suddenly roll in from the sea, covering everything with a blanket of icy grey. The addage for March rings very true on the coast, 'In like a lion, out like a lamb'. By April the weather seems to have settled. Watching adders on Salthouse Heath is one of my spring highlights. Blackthorn races to an early blossom, queen bees appear fresh out of hibernation, the reedbeds come alive with the sound of Sedge and Reed Warblers, often calling throughout the night. There's love and war in the sky over the marsh and reedbeds; Lapwings frenetic tumbling display flight and Skylarks noisy ascent to the heavens before they parachute at high speed to the ground. Marsh Harriers parry the challenges of smaller brave birds as they glide over the land. Our wintering herons and egrets can feed again from the bounty of frogs and spawn.

Blakeney Freshes April Hares   Before the devasting surge tide in December 2013, these fields were full of hares. It's sad to think that I probably photographed the soggy drowned bodies of these hares the morning after the tide (see page 38).

It looked like three amorous males were after one female. Just when you thought she'd managed to shake them off, they'd start up again and the chase continued. Skylarks and Meadow Pipits shot out of the dew-laden grass as they trundled by.

top left *Female Adder in the Grass, Salthouse* Although the weather in March is often unpredictable, a few days of sunshine always brings out the adders. As soon as this happens, I head to the Heath. Watching male adders writhe in combat has to be one of the most compelling wildlife spectacles I've ever seen. On this occasion, after finding the female, it wasn't long before a male approached. He slides over her, rapidly flicking his tongue, while she remains stock still. From the corner of my eye another male is heading straight for the courting adders. This time both males were determined to have this female.

The following battle lasts on and off around two and a half hours. The exhausted pair stop a short distance from one another. I think it's over but as soon as one approaches the female, it starts again. So focused on their battle, which involves trying to push the opponent to the ground, they completely ignore me. Finally it's over, the loser heads straight for my legs, resting in my shadow before it moves on. I freeze and it moves to the right of my foot and slips into cover. above & right *Males Adders 2.5 Hours Fighting*

6pm Sea Fret, March I shivered at my desk and wandered why the sudden change of light. From looking out of the window to grabbing my camera and arriving on the Coast Path must have been only a matter of minutes. The following hour was the most ethereal experience I've ever had on the marsh. It was as if the whole world stopped as the fret rolled in from the sea, smothering the sun and muffling all sound.

6.17pm Sea Fret, March The ghoulish light only lasted for another ten minutes or so but still, I could probably fill this book with the amount of pictures I took.

Snipe, March Harsh weather made this little brown dumpling unusually tame. I watched it and it watched me.

Snowy Reedbed, by Artemis Cafe, Cley Just when you think winter is over, March has a habit of sneaking in days of dreadful weather. Of all the months, I find March the hardest to like. It promises some of the best days for wildlife watching and the worst days for unwelcome, biting northerly winds laden with heavy and prolonged showers.

Stretching Hare, March I hadn't intended to sit in Daukes Hide until sundown, but I got involved in a Hare stand off, neither of us wanting to be the first to move on. Finally it tired of staring at me and after an epic yoga-like stretching routine and one last look, it sloped off.

above *Hare Sunset, Daukes Hide, March* After the Hare disappeared, I stayed in the hide to watch the sunset. As the light faded the orange sky began to glow, wisps of pink mist rose from the pools, hovering just above ground level making the feeding Curlews shimmer in a spooky, pearlescent light.

Towards Beau Rivage, Cley, March A damp dog blanket of a
sky, a cloying sea fret that hung around until darkness. Suddenly
the tranquility was shattered by a Cetti's Warbler's explosive,
jack-in-the-box, whack in the face, machine-fire song.

top *Sunset from Bramble Flap, April* A great place to watch Bank Voles, Minnows, Reed warblers and of course, cows.
bottom *Bad Sky, May*

top *Reedcutters Tractor with Wiveton Church, March*
left *The Olympia* The Reedcutters set up base camp by
the Cley Sluice gates when they cut this area of marsh.
It seems brutal, for Bearded Reedlings it must be like
having their home destroyed, a rainforest in miniature.
But without harvesting the reedbeds become a tangled
mess, clogged and impenetrable and of no use to the
700 species that thrive in this special habitat.

Reed Bundles, Glaven Reedbeds

Burning the Marsh, Cley NWT, March While sitting in Daukes Hide, I noticed a plume of smoke rising from the middle of the reserve. I walked along East Bank to the beach to get a better view. It must take great skill and nerves of steel to set fire to one of the oldest and best-known nature reserves in the country!

Burning Marsh, Cley Mill, March

Unbelievable Sleet Storm from Old Woman's Lane, March I don't think any photograph will ever be able to capture the drama of this storm. I'd been listening to sleet lashing the gallery windows, wondering if Rachel was getting wet on her way home. She called me and in a frantic voice told me to head to the reserve asap. I asked if she was getting soaked but incredibly the storm hadn't touched the Newgate end of the village. We sat in the car on Old Woman's Lane and watched as the end of the world sky headed out to sea.

Coastguards Cottages, Weybourne, March Another day and another sleet storm out at sea. My hands froze from the cold, I had no gloves, no hat and I think my teeth actually did chatter. March, it really is a bugger of a month.

Reeds & Slate Sky, April

Sun Spot Reeds, Cley NWT Reserve, April

New Scrape with Avocets & Shoveler Ducks, April Since the surge tide of 2013, the National Trust's Blakeney Nature Reserve has done great work restoring the freshwater marsh. These new scrapes on the Cley side of the marsh were an instant hit with many birds, especially Avocets and Redshanks who both successfully reared broods. While sitting watching the life of the pools unfold, I couldn't believe the diversity of species surrounding me on this fresh marsh.

New Scrape with Lapwing & Avocet, April At the end of a busy day, these new scrapes became the perfect place to sit quietly and watch. As well as the regular ducks and waders, other visitors enticed by the freshwater include Linnets, Meadow Pipits, Skylarks, Sparrows and Reed Buntings.

New Scrape with Avocet, Ripples &
Reflections, April

Hawthorn Glinting in the Reeds, Cley

Low Tide, Blue Light, Blakeney Bay, April The bay at low tide takes a breather before the next sudden rush of tide charges in. Waders take advantage of the vast plains of nutrient-rich mud; the vast backdrop of land and sky makes them look tiny.

Red Marsh, Halfway House The proper title for this building on Blakeney Point is The Watch House. It was built in the 1830s for the wonderfully named 'Prevention Men' an early version of Customs & Excise. From wherever I am on either the beach or marshes, I can usually see it out of the corner of my eye: a diligent sentry, standing guard over the marsh in all weathers.

Wiveton Church, Late April A walk to Wiveton Bridge to spot the 7pm Barn
Owl and check the hedgerows by the sewage works to see if the Nightingales
have arrived.

Ditch & Pump by Wiveton Church, April

top *Sedge Warbler in the Reeds* It's the end of April and the reedbeds are buzzing with life. The relentless songs of returning Sedge and Reed Warbler continues day and night, I still find their voices hard to tell apart. Egrets begin nesting and will have eggs by the end of the month. Cetti's Warblers join in too, the trickster of the reedbeds, surprising you with their explosive 'in your face' song.

above *Stretching Little Egret*

left *Chinese Water Deer* During the winter months, if I see them it's in pairs but from April onwards, they always seem to be on their own.

left & top *Long-tailed Tit & Nest*, May A trip to Salthouse Heath to see if I can find snakes. No snakes today, instead I watched a Long-tailed and Coal Tit (above) squabble in the Gorse. It took some time to find the nest, the Coat Tit quickly moved on but I stayed and watched the Long-tails tend their lichen and cobweb nest.

Red Ball Sun, Cley Beach Path, May
Emma Lynne, Cley Beach, April

Rachel's Ditch, Cley, May

Sea Fret, Daukes Hide, May By 9.30am the heat was already steaming from the land. I walked to the sea and noticed wisps of mist rising over the water in the Eye Field. In the distance, Salthouse and Weybourne were shimmering in a heat haze.
Eye Field In the Morning with Mist

Early Light, Cley Mill Some mornings you just know its going to be a special weather day.

Emma Lynne in the Mist, May Around 10am, just as people were arriving at the beach to make the most of the sun, a fret rolled in from the sea, sucking the life out of the sun. It hung over the sea and land, putting a chill into everything it touched.

Yellow Reeds Blue Water Walking towards Walsey Hills via the NWT Cley Marshes, I'm always mesmerized by the crystal clear stream that runs the length of the reserve. Vast underwater forests of towering Soft Hornwort, darting Minnows, and Sticklebacks and if you're lucky a Water Vole making a dash to the other side.

Frog Pool, March I'm amazed there are any frogs or toads left on the reserve. Everywhere you look, there's either a Heron or Little Egret hunched over the marsh, poised and ready to strike.

above   *Halfway House, from HMS Heron, April*   After checking the weather, we took our boat out from Cley Harbour to Halfway House. I find it impossible to go straight there without dropping anchor. There are so many hidden parts of the marsh to explore, all offering different views of the surrounding vastness.

top right   *Motoring Up The Glaven, May*   On another occasion, we were racing our poor little boat home to avoid getting soaked, sadly we didn't make it.

bottom right   Sailing past clumps of Suaeda and carpets of Purslane, Meadow Pipits and Curlews fly up calling out their annoyance at our presence. But all pale in comparison to the alarming racket of the Redshank, always the first to cry a warning call, earning its nickname as the 'siren of the marsh'.

left *You Dirty Rats, Salthouse, May* It's probably not high on many people's list of things to do, but visiting the rats by the duck pool is certainly up there for me. These slinky opportunists wait for a lump of bread intended for the ducks to fall, nip in, pick up and scarper.

right *Gypsy Stallion, Salthouse* While photographing the rats, from the corner of my eye I saw a Jackdaw jumping up and down on the back of the resting horse. It was busy plucking hairs from it's back, jumping every time the horse flicked its tail in annoyance, but always returning to the same spot. Eventually the horse had enough, made to bite the Jackdaw then leapt up and charged around the field.

81

Sun Up Over Sheringham from Cley Beach, 7.50am A flask of tea and a walk to the beach this morning. We'd had a few days of crisp, dry weather with bright skies but this morning was particularly still. While I sat on the beach watching the sunrise, the only sound came from the occasional wave slapping the shingle and the soft murmurrings of Brent Geese on the Eye Field.

Walking Home Past The Three Swallows, 8pm Tonight's walk home felt like we were walking in a spooky film set, we half expected to see the Dark Riders of Mordor charging out of the mist.

SUMMER

june july august

And now the madness begins. Bright lights, big colours and long days. Spring was the warm up act, now the marsh is a sea of pinks and mauves, the heath is bright cadmium yellow and marsh pools reflect the bright blue sky.

Out on the reserves, parents fight to protect their young as every predator is on the lookout for an easy meal. Avocets bully and charge anything that comes near and Blakeney Point becomes one of the biggest tern crèches in the country. Common Seal pups are born on the point and boat trips from Morston steam out there every day. Barn Owls work overtime to feed their broods, often hunting during the day and we watch as they hover and dive into the grass for voles.

Cley beach turns from a windy deserted stretch of coast to a thriving picnic and swimming venue. Fishermen line the beach in search of Mackerel and Bass, often camping overnight in their quest to catch fish.

Towards the end of the season, the shadows lengthen and the grasses begin to run out of green. Norfolk is the driest county in the UK and if it's been a hot, dry summer, the land looks brittle and exhausted. Autumn arrives and brings with it soft, warm rainfall and mists.

top *Midges and Reeds, 9.15pm*
left *Lone Cow in the Grass*

Evening Sunshine, Bramble Flap Summer is here. Lustrous reedbeds and dazzling last light. The sun falls behind the grasses, casting warm orange shadows over everything. The grasses and reeds are bursting with new life; freshly hatched birds and insects, and the tinny whine from mosquitoes.

Beach Walk Towards Sheringham, August Warm evenings, Cornflower blue sea and the shingle suffused with the warm glow of the dipping sun. I didn't want to stop walking this evening. As I crunched along the beach, Meadow Pipits appeared almost underfoot, crying 'tsip, tsip' as they bounced away.

Walking Home with Sunset Fishing, August My leg-aching walk back along the beach was rewarded with this magical scene. The peach-coloured salty spray from the sea kept me cool as I trudged home.

Fishing from Cley Beach, July & August You know when the Mackerel have arrived, the beach from Cley to Weybourne is lined with fishermen. Sea Bass come close to the beach, right in to the surf. I've seen one leap from the water to catch a gull, it missed but only just.

The warm water is not only good for fish, the beach is a popular swimming spot with locals, swimming while the sun sets is a real treat and if you're lucky, a seal will pop up to see what you're up to. I've seen some ridiculous sunsets from the beach in August but the one top left has to be the best yet.

Sea Lavender, High Tide From July the summer marsh is covered in vast swathes of seaside candy pink. As the tide started to cover the warm marsh, I couldn't resist taking off my socks and shoes to wade through. I didn't fall this time but I've been caught out before by a hidden underwater pool, lying in wait to catch enthusiastic photographers.

top *Submerged Sea Lavender, Cley Mill, August* From July to October the marsh colours are turned up to eleven: lurid green, cobalt blue, lilac, magenta and mauve. bottom *Lone Boat, Morston* and *Sea Lavender* From Cley to Morston, the marsh is covered with insect feeding bees on the flowers.

Watching The Tide Fill the Summer Marsh A lazy hour sitting
and watching the incoming tide swirl and eddy across the
marsh, rushing to fill pools. The land smells of seaweed and
summer drains, briny with a hint of antiseptic too.

Stretching Juvenile Coot, June and *Emerging Emporer Dragonfly* There's new life everywhere I look.

Shelduck & Avocet Squabbles, June It's a lively time of year on the scrapes now. Parents are busy protecting territory and young, Marsh Harriers float over the reserve on the lookout for stray chicks, and Shelducks and Avocets are forever bickering. I watched as an interloping Shelduck upset its fellow kin, but as soon as an Avocet strayed too close, they stopped squabbling amongst themselves and all three turned on the poor bird. But it's hard to sympathise with the Avocet, they're an aggressive bird, incredibly intolerant to anything else sharing their space - I've even seen them take on a swan.

top *Oystercatchers & Rabbits, Eye Field, Cley* A walk to the beach this morning before work; I should have been rushing back to open the gallery, but watching the rabbits' stamping and mock charges made me late this morning.

above *Bramble Flap Kestrel* There are two that live by the gate; one of them is usually there to say hello to in the morning. It's near here that they like to ambush the Barn Owl if it's carrying a vole.

Norfolk Coast Path near Cley Mill, August From June to August the noisy biodiversity is in full swing along the footpath. Birds are everywhere; Linnets, Goldfinches, Reed Buntings, Common Whitethroats and Sparrows thrive in the path margins. As well as birds, insect life also thrives; grasshoppers, butterflies, spiders and moths.

top to bottom *Reed Warbler, Sedge Warbler Adult, Sedge Warbler Juvenile, Grasshopper Warbler* Sadly I haven't seen a Grasshopper Warbler on the Freshes for the last two years. Although incredibly hard to see, this one reeled away its insect song until late in the evening, indifferent to me and my camera.

above *Rain on the Reserve, August, 8am* A claggy morning but with the promise of better weather to come. I walked to the beach through a blanket of warm rain with the sun trying to push through the cloud all the way. When it finally happened, it was like a giant spotlight, illuminating sections of the marsh in turn.

right *Towards Weybourne Camp from Walsey Hills* and *Towards Blakeney Point from Walsey Hills* The view from our 'hill' in Cley always amazes me, everything looks both vast and small all at once. It's owned by the Norfolk Ornithological Association and as well as spectacular views of Cley and Salthouse Marshes, it is a good watchpoint for migrating birds.

left *Chinese Water Deer Hiding in the Grass, Blakeney, July* Walking from Cley to Blakeney on the Coastal Path in July, the lushness of the grasses are always worth scanning. This morning a rather obliging ginger deer with teddy bear ears was tiptoeing through the grass.

above *Rosebay Willowherb, Blakeney, July*

103

From East Bank, near Arnold's Marsh, June A evening walk looping NWT Cley
Marshes. There's a very different feel to this area of the reserve. The colours of
Arnold's Marsh remind me of the Camargue but instead of Flamingos, Little Egrets
dot the scrape along with good numbers of wading birds, especially the Audrey
Hepburn of waders, the Avocet.

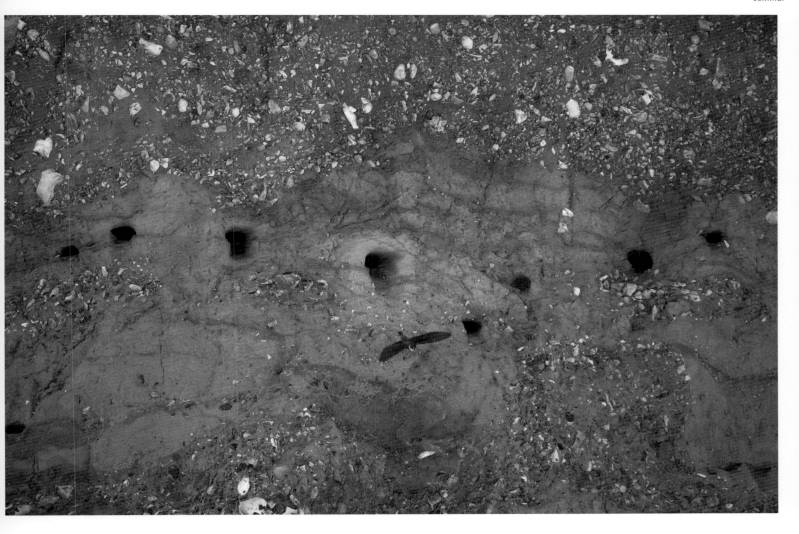

Sand Martins Golden Bank, Gramborough Hill, Salthouse, August I can still feel my neck burning from taking this picture. It took a while and many bad photos to get this shot as they kept flying out too quickly. But 'guess the hole' has now become my favourite beach game. In the end, I picked one hole and waited. But what a wait – blue sky, blue sea and an abundance of butterflies floating down from the hill.

105

Mad Sky, from Salthouse Heath, August

Sand Hills Sundown, Blakeney Point, August

The Old Lifeboat Station, Blakeney Point, August The colours kept changing with every blink of the eye this evening. In the end, I stopped walking, made a nest in the grass and watched the whole sunset unfold.

Red Sky & Pools, Blakeney Point, August

Passing Blakeney Bay, Coast Path, August I can't think of anywhere else I'd rather be on a summer's evening when it's like this. The marsh had been baked by the sun all day and as the air cooled, you could almost hear the land sigh with relief.

Shimmering Boats, Blakeney Bay, August Cranking my zoom lens to the max and aiming straight for the sun (and probably ruining my eyes in the process) the view looked more like an oil painting than a photograph. I walked home at 9pm in a t-shirt and was still warm by the time I got home.

111

above *Cley Footpath, July* The footpaths and verges around Cley are left to grow wild. The Environment Agency cuts the Coast Path back in September, if they do it sooner, precious late summer food for birds and invertebrates is lost. above right *Alexanders Against the Sun*

opposite page *Seedheads, Cley, late August* Heading towards autumn, long shadows and floating, snow-like thistle seeds catch the wind. right The distinctive black seeds of Alexanders line the hedgerows and paths. Look closely and you can see Araneus spiders laying eggs in silken cocoons to keep them safe until the following May. She wont survive the winter, the first frosts will kill her.

below *Red Legged Partridge Family & Straggler*
While photographing the path, I hadn't seen the partridge hiding in the grasses right in front of my foot. The chicks came out of hiding and walked almost over my toes.

top *Crab Jetty, Morston, July* A typical day in July in North Norfolk: blue sky, grey sky, no wind, lots of wind, rain and a smattering of sleet for good measure. left *Redshank with Very Red Shanks* Wherever you walk on the marshes, the marsh siren will always be there, alerting all and sundry that you're about to seriously ruin their day.

top *Morning Mist, Salthouse, August* There's a special atmosphere or energy on Salthouse's heath and marshes, it's hard to explain but walking there on your own, especially at dusk, is the best way to experience it. right *Red Moon & Blue Mist, Salthouse, August* One minute I was scanning the field for Whimbrel when a blue mist appeared from nowhere. This would have been enough to make my day but then a big red moon lifted out of the horizon, thinking about that evening still gives me goosebumps.

AUTUMN

september october november

It's as if the seasons have been preparing all year for its finale. The dazzling colours of summer ebb away, long shadows and swathes of warm glowing light bathe the land. Who better than Keats could describe autumn: 'stubble plains with rosy hue and soft-dying days'. The 'season of mists' is by far my favourite time to take pictures and as Cley is surrounded by marshes and reedbeds, the atmosphere can be magical.

There's change everywhere you look around Cley. Our summer visiting birds have gone home but newbies are moving in. The first Pink-footed and Brent Geese are heard high in the sky and birdwatchers get excited as rare migrants are blown off course and drop to our reserves. The reedbeds turn from a sea of gold to a fog of bruised purple. This is the best time to see and hear noisy groups of Bearded Reedlings 'ting, tinging' through the reeds.

The hedgerows turn Christmas red and green with fruiting Hawthorns and blue-black Sloe Berries cover the Blackthorn hedges. Winter thrushes gorge in preparation for the winter and large flocks of Golden Plovers, Lapwings and Starlings gather in the fields.

6am Halfway House, Blakeney Point, September Even though its proper name is The Watch House, I've always called it Halfway House as it used to be half way when walking to the Point from Cley Beach. But the shifting sands have made this spit of shingle longer now, so it isn't half way anymore. Perhaps it should be called 'Quarter Way House'.

top *Sunrise near Pinchen's Creek, Blakeney Point*
bottom *Sundown Behind the Sand Hills, Blakeney Point*

Sunrise from Halfway House, September 1st Sitting on the beach wrapped in a blanket clutching a cup of tea, the rest of the world seems a very long way away. The soundtrack this morning - an orchestra of bird chatter from the Pit, bubbling 'ker-lee' calls from a Curlew and the slapping lap of waves on the shingle.

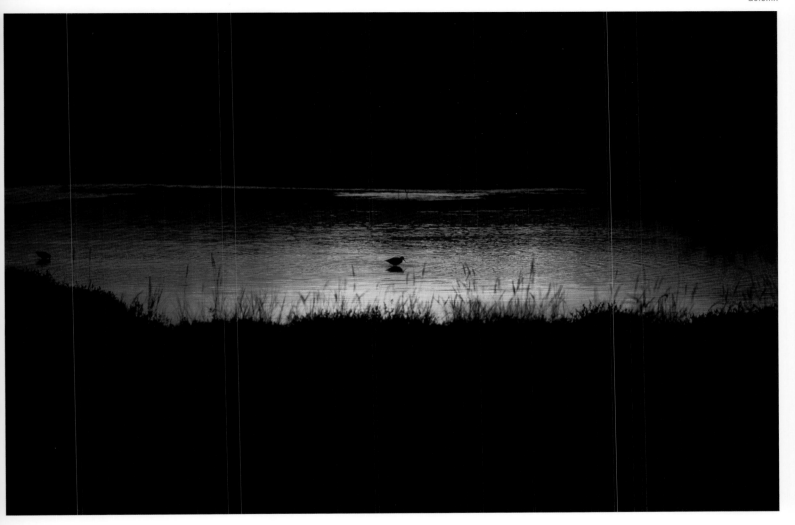

Orange Water with Redshanks, 1st October From awesome sunrises to glowing sunsets. Walking on the marsh at the end of the day, watching the creeks turn orange and the grasses black.

left *Soft Morning Reeds, Cley, November*
left *Sparkling Reedbed, Cley*
right *Bearded Reedling Family, October*
I will never tire of watching these noisy ginger acrobats work through the reeds. Also known as Bearded Tits, I normally hear them first, their frantic, metallic sounding 'tee-u, tee-u' calls, like tinny bell chimes ringing through the reeds. Sometimes I see them on the path, picking up grit; they change diet once the insects have gone and need the grit to help their digestion. They're amazing and probably our most exotic-looking native bird in the UK.

A Tit In The Reeds, November Watching Blue Tits in the reeds always seems a bit incongruous to me, but it's probably one of the species I see the most. In autumn, when the Bearded Reedling family groups are at their noisiest, there's usually a group of Blue Tits nearby.

right *Grazing Cows by Bramble Flap, September*
right *Pregnant Cow, Bramble Flap, September*
I always keep an eye on the lowering sun this time of
year. If it looks good, I make a dash to this location. The
cows here tend to come to this field late in the afternoon
and if all the conditions are correct, the backlit sun gives
them that 'Ready Brek' radioactive orange glow.

Winter Reeds Blue Water, November
Pioneering Reeds, October
Birder's Beach Hotel, Cley Beach, November

Bright blue autumn days. The brightness of summer but with crispy 'auto white balance' light. Walking around the NWT's Cley Marshes, ending up at the Beach Car Park and another of Cley's iconic buildings.

Coot in Weed, September
Migrant Hawker, September
Blue Marsh Pools, September

SS Vera & Gull, Cley Beach, October I set out in sunshine and came home in a storm. The invading cloud came in from the west, as if a giant blind was being drawn across the sky. In 1914 the cargo ship SS Vera collided with the Parthian and sank. At low tide you can still it poking out of the sea.

Gull Roost from Daukes Hides, 6.15am, September
The Reedbed by Artemis Cafe, 8.05am, October

Red Bay at Night, Blakeney, September We had the offer of an evening sail with
friends in the Bay. In fact, it turned out to be an evening of sitting on the water and
not moving; what little wind we had dropped completely, leaving us to gently drift
with the tide, relax and watch the sun go down.

Beach Road Pools, Cley, October Walking home from the beach, I always stop at these pools to see who's there. Normally there are Redshanks, Black-headed Gulls, a Curlew or two and if I'm lucky, a Little Egret.

Pink-footed Geese, Cley, October Waking up to the squeaky excited honks of my favourite geese piling into Norfolk is the wildlife highlight of my year. We're surrounded by tens of thousands of these exquisite geese who come to Norfolk every winter from their breeding grounds in Iceland & Greenland. Watching the sky darken as thousands come into land in a wild goose cacophony is an experience never to be forgotten.

Starlings on Cley Mill & Starlings in Picnic Fayre Car Park, October Starlings start to form large chattering, whistling flocks, murmurations, a delicious word to say. Just before dark, they sit on the mill, as if to catch up on the gossip of the day before going to roost. Noisily, they burst out of the reeds, fly up fast then drop down out of sight. They stop calling all at once and suddenly, all is quiet in the reedbed.

Sunrise over Cley Reedbeds, October   As I took this picture, a family of around
ten Bearded Reedlings 'ting ting' called their way towards me. I was rewarded
with an intimate Bearded Reedling experience before breakfast.

River Glaven with Wiveton Church, November   I crunched my way through the frost-coated grass this morning. As I took the picture, a startled Heron gracefully lifted from water, making me jump and take a picture of the sky.

Redwing in the Mist, October An unusual visitor this morning on the Coast Path; a thrush grounded by the fog flicked through the Alexanders. I was hoping for a rare American migrant, a Waterthrush perhaps? But no, a beautiful Redwing instead.

Cow in the Mist, September

Rachel's Ditch in the Mist, September

Rainbow, Cley,
The George, Cley
Sunrise over Cley Mill,
Three pictures of Cley showing the randomness of weather during autumn. I took the picture of the Rainbow while getting a real drenching, I'm amazed the camera survived.

Halfway House from Cley Beach, October A wispy pink mist hovered over the marsh as I walked to the beach this evening. The sea became turquoise blue as the orange sky set, you could be forgiven for thinking you're in the Caribbean on nights like these.

Sudden Storm Over Cley, September I set out in the sunshine with my mum's dog this morning. I could see a bank of grey storm clouds racing towards me, but I was too distracted photographing the high tide and enjoying the dramtic light. Needless to say I got completely soaked and the dog shivered and whimpered all the way home – she still hasn't forgiven me.

Summer Breeze, Blakeney Point, September A day spent out on the sandbanks between tides. The seals' woeful moaning calls carrying across the sands, clouds skudding over the endless view. Is this really England?

141

top *Sunlight Sandbanks, Blakeney Point, October*
bottom *From Juno, Blakeney Point, October*

Low Tide, Blakeney Point, October Out on the far reaches of Blakeney Point at low tide, looking towards Stiffkey and Wells, it feels like you're the only person left in the world. With only the seals and seabirds for company, this is wilderness at its best.

SARAH WHITTLEY
I was born in Norwich and brought up in Norfolk. When I was eighteen I moved to London to try and start a career in publishing. My first job was an editorial assistant with Chapman & Hall Publishers. After becoming a junior commissioning editor, I left to join a publishing firm back in Norwich, working as a general editor. Next I set up The Wildlife Art Agency, an international illustration agency, representing over 50 illustrators, supplying artwork, design and book concepts to major publishers.

In 2005 I moved to Cley and opened The Pinkfoot Gallery (named after the goose). The gallery specialises in contemporary art with a special interest in art inspired by nature. www.pinkfootgallery. co.uk. And in 2011 I started my own publishing company to make beautiful Scribblers and books and about art, wildlife and Norfolk. www.redharepublishing.co.uk

I have written several natural history books and collectively worked on many more. My latest book is called Despicable Bugs and you can find out more from www.despicablebooks.com

My Twitter account follows my photographic journey around North Norfolk @SarahWhittley and Instagram @Redhares

BUYING PRINTS
If you'd like to buy any of the pictures from this book please contact me directly: sarahwhittley@icloud.com. The pictures come in a variety of formats, including large canvases over stretchers o printed with Giclee inks on watercolour paper.

My photographs are on show and are for sale a Artemis Homes & Antiques in Cley: info@artemisantiques.co.uk www.artemisantiques.co.uk & Twitter @artemiscafe

THANK YOU
Thank you Rachel for proofing my text and looking through endless pictures with me – you've the patience of a saint! And George fo your proofing too. Jody for photo-editing help, Sophie for showing my photos in her shop and Alex for the great coffee. And Robin Chittenden for teaching me how to use a camera many years ago Thanks to The National Trust Blakeney Reserve and The Norfolk Wildlife Trust for all their hard work protecting our valuable habitats www.nationaltrust.org.uk/blakeney and www.norfolkwildlifetrust org.uk. Not forgetting www.noa.org.uk & www.norfolkreed.co.uk

And thank you Mike Dawson from Swallowtail Print for all your help and, of course, your fabulous printing www.swallowtailprint.co.uk